TECTONIC PLATES
HOW THE WORLD CHANGED

An Elementary Introduction to World-Wide Tectonic Plate Migrations Over 750 Million Years

CW01335822

Dr Peter Roberts
BSc MSc PhD

First Edition November 2016

Published in the United Kingdom
by
Russet Publishing
russetpublishing.com

Distributed internationally through
Book Depository, Amazon, Barnes & Noble, Waterstones, etc.
by
Lulu Press Inc.
Durham, North Carolina, USA
lulu.com

Printed Version
ISBN 978-1-910537-21-3
Not available as an electronic version

Comments and corrections welcome to
peter.roberts@russetpublishing.com

- - - - - - - oOo - - - - - - -

Also, see *"Historical Geology in Maps"*.
Maps of the Past Geology, Geography, Coastlines,
and Climate of the British Isles and Ireland.
It includes all the tectonic plate maps from this book and is
available from bookdepository.com, amazon.com, amazon.co.uk, Barnes
and Noble, Waterstones, etc.

About the author

Dr Roberts obtained his Bachelor's degree from the University of Nottingham in geology, with subsidiary studies in physics, geography, pedology, climatology, meteorology, and oceanography. He obtained his Master's and Doctorate from the University of Salford.

Before he retired, his career was as a consulting geotechnical engineer and geologist, working extensively throughout the U.K. as well as abroad. He was a Visiting Professor at a British University for over ten years. He is the author of several textbooks and more than one hundred published papers.

His more-recently published geotechnical books may be viewed at russetpublishing.com

Or you can go directly to russetpublishing.com/geotechnology if you wish.

Acknowledgments

I thank my wife, Helena, for her great help in preparing all the text and figures for this book. She put in a prodigious amount of work typing the text and preparing all the figures and tables using Apple's Graphic© software - and she did an amazing job.

And I would particularly thank her for her endless, cheerful interest in my work. I literally could not have produced this book without her.

Thank you so much.

I would also like to thank the various authors of detailed, knowledgeable, and authoritative textbooks and published research papers whose work I read during the production of my small book to keep myself up-to-date. For a more detailed study of British palaeogeographical changes, I recommend the short reading list at the end of this book. My work is just an introductory approximation compared to their wonderful detail, which is clearly needed for any professional purposes.

About this book

The object of this book is to simplify a complex and very specialised subject so that it can be presented clearly and briefly.

With simplification comes approximation designed to permit rapid learning and understanding. Including more detail in the book would be easy, but distilling the essential tectonic plate configuration for each major geological period is difficult.

This book presents fourteen briefly-explained **plate migration maps** of the entire globe, showing the approximated movements and positions of the world's major tectonic plates over the last 750 million years. This gives "the big picture", explaining how and why our climate has changed so radically with time.

The plate locations have been drawn onto a new type of stylised projection for both clarity and continuity from one map to the next. Many books use varying projections, which make the sequence of movements more difficult to follow.

This book has been written and the maps drawn for beginners, night classes, schools, universities, amateur geologists, climatologists and even for professional geologists.

This book is for anyone who wants to understand the causes of the huge changes in the world's geology, oceans, and climate, which have, in turn, created and moulded its diverse geographical landscapes.

Note to the reader

This book provides a useful background to long-term global climate change, using which the magnitude and causes of current global warming may be considered and assessed.

This is the exciting story of the evolution of the continents and oceans of our planet, illustrated in a series of simplified, systematic maps for easy reference.

Caveat

This work is published for personal interest and general information purposes only. In its preparation, a considerable amount of interpretation, and opinion has necessarily been used. It should NOT be relied upon for professional works or situations of responsibility. For such purposes, refer to the reading list provided at the end of this book, and other authoritative works. All the maps are broad approximations, significantly simplified to aid the beginner in understanding the development of our continents and oceans over time.

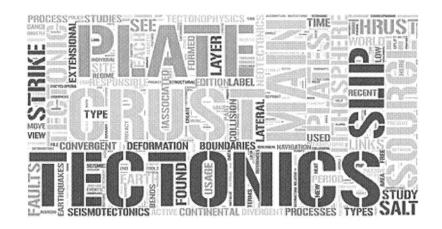

A Brief Introduction to Plate Tectonics

Many people who are new to geology wonder how we can tell how old rocks are.

They also want to know what sort of evidence we use to work out how the tectonic plates have migrated around the world. How do we know where plates were millions of years ago?

So, here are some FAQs (Frequently Asked Questions) and some approximate answers.

FAQ: *How can geologists tell how old rocks are?*

Answer: We know that unstable radioactive minerals are incorporated included in basalt and granite rocks when they form, and we know the rate at which those minerals decay from being radioactive to becoming stable. Therefore, we use special instruments to measure how much radioactivity is left, and from that we can assess the age of igneous rocks.

We can measure radioactive decay quite accurately, but sometimes other subsequent geological activities such as mountain building metamorphism can disturb the original chemistry of rocks and alter their radioactive status. So we can sometimes be uncertain about an igneous rock's age.

We can also use our common sense and observation to tell whether other rocks are older than or younger than the igneous rocks we have dated. For example, if a dated dolerite is intruded into a limestone, then clearly that limestone is older than the dolerite. And so we can create approximate tables of the ages of other types of rocks as well.

FAQ: *How can we know where the crustal plates were hundreds of millions of years ago?*

Answer: We can only assess - almost guess - where they were by using indirect information such as the type of rocks being deposited on a plate's crust. For example, if a continent on a plate has desert rocks forming during the Permian, then we can guess that it was just north or south of the equator during that period because that's where we find deserts such as the Sahara or the Kalahari today.

Alternatively, we could find features related to ice and glaciers and we could suggest that the plate may have been in the region of the South Pole at that time, for example. We make lots of rough guesses and some more accurate ones and then we use scientific lithological, mineralogical, and palaeontological tests to confirm our hypotheses. Slowly we can use them all to create a slightly more reliable picture.

FAQ: *What makes the crustal plates move over the surface of the world?*

Answer: We believe that below the Earth's crust there exists a dense, very viscous, semi-liquid material called 'magma'. The upper zone of this magma is called the mantle. When magma cools at the Earth's surface, it solidifies to form igneous rocks, creating crustal plates with lighter minerals forming continents on top of them. So the crustal plates float on top of the mantle.

At some places in the mantle, radioactive decay of minerals generates heat differentially, which warms the magma so that it becomes less dense and starts to rise towards the surface. The rising magma spreads out when it reaches the base of the solidified crust, and travels laterally towards cooler places, where it sinks once more. These are called convection currents. The lateral spread of the magma beneath the base of the crust is the most likely mechanism for dragging the plates along over the planet's surface. Where plates are driven into each other, one of them is usually forced under the other, forming what is called a 'subduction zone'. That lower plate is destroyed by melting, whilst the upper plate is crumpled to form a rising mountain chain.

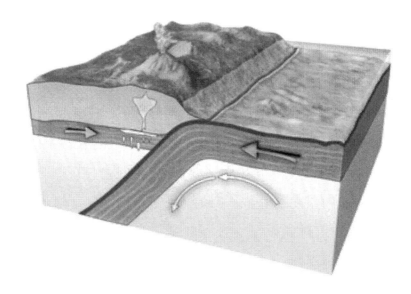

The following two diagrams show how extremely rocks can be distorted by the mountain-building forces exerted over subduction zones.

Where two plates are being dragged apart, magma rises, reaching the surface. Then it cools, forming a new, solid 'spreading margin' between the two plates. In the two photographs below, you can see the very rare existence of a spreading margin that can be examined on land. It is in Iceland in the North Atlantic Ocean, where the American and Eurasian plates are being pulled apart.

There are plenty of volcanoes and lava flows in the vicinity, as a result of the tension in the Earth's crust.

Sometimes - over very long periods of time - the areas of heating and cooling change, and thus the direction of drag on the base of the plates can change. The continents that form on top of the plates just move along as the plates move, and are similarly destroyed at subduction zones or built up into mountain chains.

FAQ: *Who discovered that plates move, and when?*

Answer: A gentleman called A. Snider, as far back as 1858, noticed the possibility that South America and Africa may have once been attached structurally. This is considered to be the first publication of the concept that continents may have moved.

A. Snider's published maps of 1858.

Later, in the early 20th Century, a German geophysicist and meteorologist called Alfred Wegener also realised that continents may have moved; he made this public in 1912 and called it "Continental Drift". Later, in the 1960's this was developed to include the concept of rigid, interlocking 'plates' lying on the viscous molten mantle, and being destroyed at some margins and created at others. This is 'Plate Tectonics'.

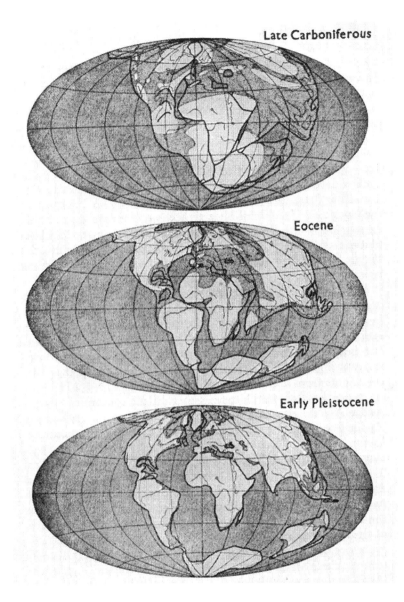

Late Carboniferous

Eocene

Early Pleistocene

Wegener's 1915 publication in "Die Entstehung der Kontinente und Ozzeane".

7

The continents form on top of the rigid plates, of which today there are about eight, with a number of minor ones as well. They are moving at rates of between zero and seventeen centimetres a year. That does not sound much, but at ten centimetres a year, a plate will travel a metre in ten years, and a hundred kilometres in a million years. So, it is easy to realise that, over hundreds of millions of years, the continents can move all over the face of the world - and they have done just that! Of course, we do not know how fast the plates moved in the past - they may have moved either faster or slower at different times - but with modern surveying equipment and the use of satellites, we can measure today's rates. Some of these rates are shown on Plate Migration Map 13.

FAQ: *What is the mechanism driving tectonic plate migration?*

Answer: Originally, molten magma was exposed at the surface of the planet all over - and then it slowly cooled down by surface heat loss, and the layer of cool rock formed the future tectonic plates.

But originally it may have looked rather like a whole series of independent small rock floes (using an analogy with ice on the sea), jostling around on the surface of the molten magma as shown in the photograph below.

Eventually, though, and naturally, the entire surface of the planet cooled down sufficiently to form a continuous skin of rock floating on the magma below. If you look at a video film of lava pouring down the side of a volcano, you will see that the red-hot lava underneath is covered by a skim of black cooled rock that floats on its surface. For whatever reason, the cooled outer surface of the lava floats on top of the lava. You and I have seen that with our own eyes via television. Well, this is what the whole world looked like at one early point in time.

You will also have observed in video films that the black solidified lava moves with the lava, as the lava flows along.

And this is basically similar to the mechanism that geologists put forward today to conjecture a driving force for the tectonic plates.

If we move on to a much larger scale, and go back in time to the point when the whole Earth became covered in a layer of black cooled rock many kilometres deep, then we can expect that this layer of black, cooled rock would act as a 'blanket', insulating the magma beneath from the cold atmosphere or oceans above.

Beneath the cooled rock (which we can think of as a 'plate' because it was newly formed and relatively thin compared to the radius of the Earth), the magma started to develop convection currents. This is a simple response, obeying the laws of physics, suggesting that the convection currents assist in the heat loss by bringing fresh, hot magma near to the Earth's surface to cool. We are all aware that liquids lose heat by means of convection currents, and so that is a second thing that we can observe as a fact. As we know, in our houses in cold countries, heat comes off the radiators by convection - the air in contact with the radiator is warmed, and rises in the form of a convection current of hot air.

So, the warm convection currents from the deeper parts of the asthenosphere and mantle rise upwards and when they meet the cool, solid crust at the top, they naturally spread out and move sideways.

We have rock plates floating on top of laterally moving magma, so the plates tend to be pulled along by friction between them and the underlying, moving magma. It is straightforward. That is the prime driving force mechanism that we conjecture today.

The result of all this is that at those places where the magma rises and spreads out, the tension on the rock plates is so great that the crust splits and starts to move apart. The gap is rapidly filled by molten magma upwelling from below, cooling, and forming more rock. We call this new rock 'oceanic plate' material.

Where horizontally moving magma streams converge, the moving plates floating on them are forced together. The forces imposed on the plates cause one of the plates to plunge down below the other one to form a subduction zone. This is not caused by the rock cooling and sinking, but is caused by the lateral force imposed on the plates as they are driven together.

One plate of rock is thrust downwards and is heated and dissolved, whilst the other plate is crumpled and rises upwards, forming mountains with erupting volcanoes and igneous intrusions.

Below, you can see a diagram showing how the Indian plate moved northwards to collide with Asia, and was forced downwards to form a subduction zone, creating the Himalayas.

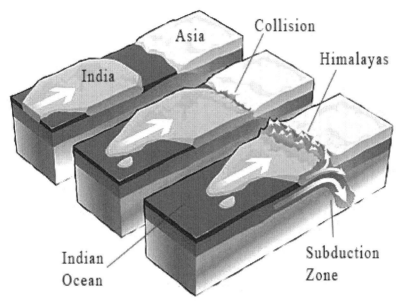

Interestingly, earthquakes can be plotted seismically in subduction zones, showing the slope and depth before the lower plunging plate becomes softened and dissolved. Published graphs and diagrams on the Internet show that the subducted plate reaches around 400 km down before it becomes sufficiently melted that it hardly generates any more earthquakes as it is dragged down. And another graph shows that the subducted plate will drag down the 1400 deg.C. isotherm from its normal horizontal level at 300 km below the surface to 600 km below the surface as the plate heats up and thus cools the surrounding magma in the process.

List of Plate Migration Maps

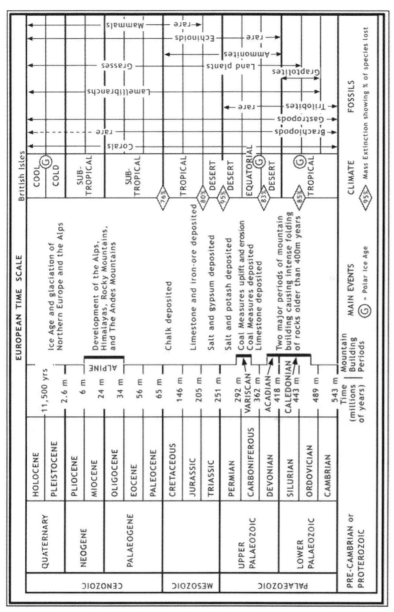

European Chronology showing Periods and Events.

13

PLATE MIGRATION MAPS
Global Plate Movements

WORLD-WIDE TECTONIC PLATE
MIGRATIONS OVER 750 MILLION YEARS

These maps form a sequential conceptualisation of the movement of the Earth's main tectonic plates over the last 750 million years. The term 'conceptualisation' is really an apology for the lack of accuracy and reliability that is represented in a sequence of maps that has been assembled from the works of a number of authors who, through diligence, have incorporated vast amounts of diverse information in their publications. It has thus been necessary to simplify and approximate in order to provide an initial skeleton framework on which the reader may subsequently place palaeogeographical details, and proceed to study them within an understandable context.

These simplified maps are intended to provide that context, and it is hoped that they will prove to be useful. In particular, this sequence of migration maps is at its most realistic in its depiction of the latitude of the Avalonian Plate, which contains most of England, and Ireland, and all of Wales. The latitudinal position of the plate accounts substantially for the climatic changes experienced over time, as reflected in the rock types found today. Avalonia's position relative to the Laurentian Plate is also depicted reasonably realistically, since the whole of Scotland and Northern Ireland is derived from that plate. The reader will observe a small icon on the Avalonian Plate representing the southern British Isles and southern Ireland. Similarly, a small icon representing Scotland and northern Ireland is drawn on the Laurentian Plate. The Early Devonian map (No 6) shows the two eventually joining together some 418 million years ago. Prior to that, the lithological and biological features of the two were fundamentally different.

14

From Devonian times onwards, once united, the geological development of Scotland, Ireland, and England was the same.

The projection used is not one with any particular scientific property, but was pragmatically constructed to give a useful representation of the areas of the planet over which the plate movements have taken place. One of the main objectives of this work has been to place the palaeogeographical representations of different authors onto a standardised single projection; each author has chosen his own 'optimum' view of different periods, with a consequent difficulty for readers to follow from one to another. Thus, 'standardisation' of view, at least, has been achieved, to the benefit of the reader.

Before looking at the map sequence, readers should familiarise themselves with the names and significance of the main tectonic plates involved. They should recognise the main theme over 750 million years as follows: During the late Pre-Cambrian, various southerly-moving plates coalesced to form the super-continent of Gondwana, which settled over our present south polar and South-Pacific regions for an immensely long period. Then Gondwana started to move back north during the late Devonian, combining with Laurasia to form the single super-continent of Pangaea during the Permian. Finally, during the Jurassic, even the mighty Pangaea broke up as the Americas started to drift westwards to form our present Atlantic Ocean. Thus, we came to the present distribution of landmasses. It is a simple story, which is told visually in the following thirteen Plate Migration maps.

For convenience of description, I refer to the left hand side of the projection as the 'western hemisphere' and the right hand side as the 'eastern hemisphere'.

In the map titles and within the text occasionally, I abbreviate the term "Million Years Before Present" into "Ma BP".

15

Map 1. Pre-Cambrian 750 Million Years Ago (Ma BP)

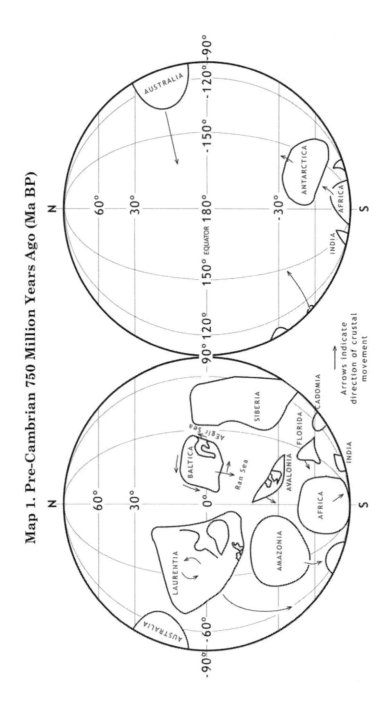

16

Plate Migration Map 1.
Pre-Cambrian 750 Million Years Ago (Ma BP)

Surprisingly, we see a plate distribution with some very vague, and coincidental similarities to the present day. But at this time, the various plates were moving southwards in the western hemisphere, passing across the south pole, and subsequently travelling northwards into the eastern hemisphere, which had been, prior to this, empty of any significant continental land masses. Both Laurentia and Baltica were rotating anti-clockwise as they travelled southwards.

Notice on Plate Migration Map 1 opposite, that the Laurentia and Avalonia plates have a very approximate outline of the northern and southern parts of the future British Isles and Ireland drawn on them.

(They ultimately meet up in the Early Devonian, as shown in Plate Migration Map 6).

Map 2. Late Pre-Cambrian 550 Million Years Ago (Ma BP)

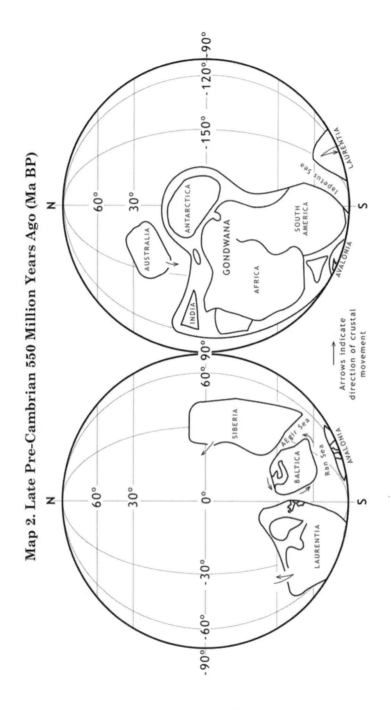

Arrows indicate
direction of crustal
movement

18

Plate Migration Map 2.
Pre-Cambrian 550 Million Years Ago (Ma BP)

By this time, most of the plates on the planet had grouped together in the eastern hemisphere, to form a super-continent that we now call Gondwana. It comprised the present-day continents of Africa, South America, India, Antarctica, Australia, and Arabia, as well as the Florida and Avalonia plates. Avalonia was joined onto the southern-most margin of Gondwana. Only Laurentia, Baltica, and Siberia remained separate.

Gondwana was destined to be a single continent lasting more than 338 million years until Jurassic times. During this period, when it was not stationary, it moved as a single fused plate.

Knowing that the Gondwana continent lasted for so long helps geologists to compare previously-shared climate and biological events across todays separate land masses. For example, the same Carboniferous glaciation can be observed in Australia, India, South America, and South Africa, even though they have now been separated greatly as a result of tectonic plate migration. Similarly, identical fossils can be identified in west Africa and eastern South America.

At the time shown in Migration Map 2 opposite, the earlier southward drift had ceased, Gondwana had become stationary, and Laurentia, Baltica, and Siberia had started to move northwards again.

Map 3. Early Cambrian 543 Million Years Ago (Ma BP)

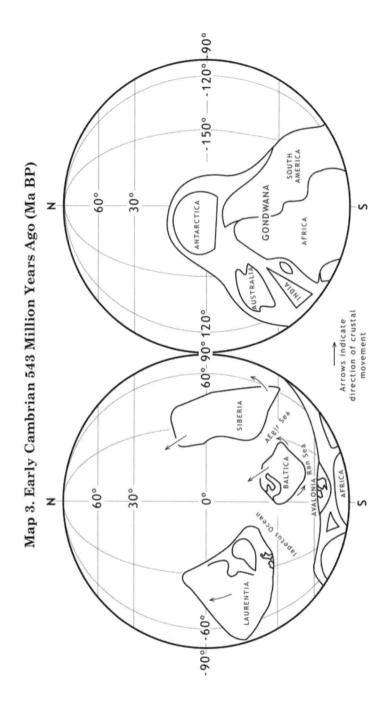

Arrows indicate direction of crustal movement

Map 3. Plate Migration
Early Cambrian 543 Million Years Ago (Ma BP)

It would seem that the Mantle convection currents that had created Gondwana and moved it southwards were now reversing, such that the plate stopped moving, whilst Laurentia, Baltica, and Siberia continued their northward journey back up the western hemisphere, rotating anti-clockwise all the while.

Avalonia was still attached to the coastal fringe of Gondwana, trapping the Florida plate between South America and Africa. Gondwana covered the South Pole and spread up over the eastern hemisphere beyond the equator. What is now the Antarctic continent would then have been experiencing tropical conditions, as would parts of Siberia and Laurentia.

The widening Iapetus Ocean, the AEgir Sea and the Ran Sea were the 'birthplace' of the newly-evolving marine creatures with exoskeleton carapaces, such as trilobites, and shelled creatures, such as brachiopods and gastropods.

The planet's atmosphere increased in carbon dioxide levels throughout the Cambrian, and global temperatures increased accordingly. At this time no animals or plants lived on the land. Prior to the evolution of land plants, erosion rates would be extremely high, and the formation of anything resembling a modern topsoil would be impossible.

It is difficult for a modern person to imagine a temperate or tropical environment without vegetation or soil-forming organisms. Warm and very wet, without a single tree or shrub, and no grass to stabilise the inorganic sand and clay produced by weathering. The logical consequence of high erosion rates is high deposition rates in shallow continental shelf marine environments - ideal for fossilisation of the new life forms.

Map 4. Early Ordovician 489 Million Years Ago (Ma BP)

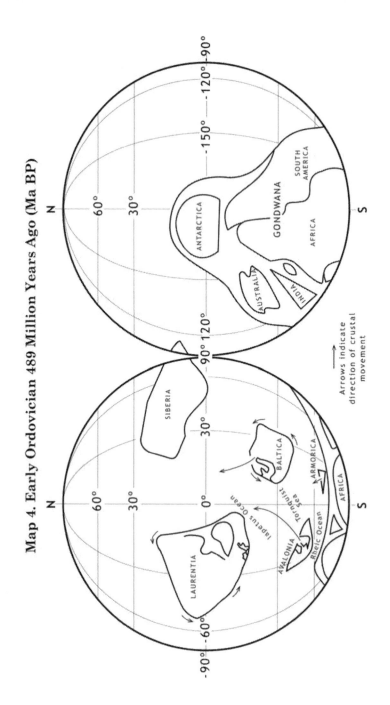

Arrows indicate
direction of crustal
movement

22

Map 4. Plate Migration
Early Ordovician 489 Million Years Ago (Ma BP)

At the end of the Cambrian, Laurentia was already moving northwards away from the South Pole plate cluster, and by Early Ordovician times, still rotating anti-clockwise, it had moved northwards to span the equator. After this, it remained stationary while Avalonia broke away from Gondwana and accelerated northwards to close on Laurentia, narrowing the Iapetus Ocean.

This meant that present day England and southern Ireland were closing northwards onto the Scottish part of the present U.K. and Northern Ireland.

While Gondwana remained stationary, Siberia moved northwards past the equator, followed ever more rapidly by Avalonia moving towards Laurentia, which itself continued to rotate anti-clockwise, approaching its present orientation as North America.

To the south of Avalonia the Rheic Ocean opened up as the Iapetus Ocean narrowed, and the Ran Sea simply disappeared, to be replaced by the Tornquist Sea, as Baltica moved away to the north, also rotating to its present orientation.

During the course of the Ordovician, the Iapetus Ocean gap closed to about 800 km, with consequent mountain building and thrusting on the SE margin of the Laurentian Plate, while on the north-west margin of Avalonia, the Scottish mountains were forming. The Southern Uplands Subduction Zone swallowed up the closing plates, with the consequent production of volcanic activity and plutonic intrusive placement.

Map 5. Early Silurian 443 Million Years Ago (Ma BP)

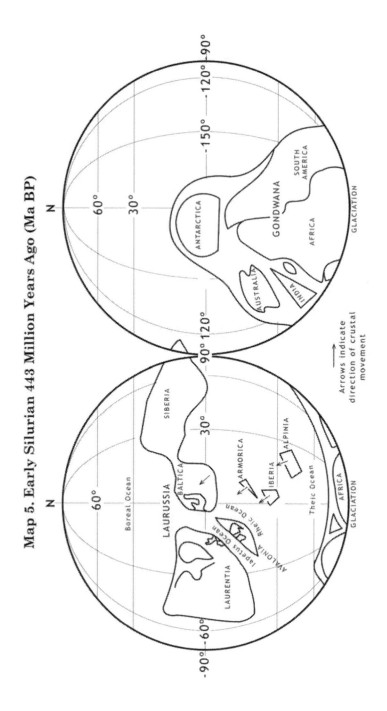

Map 5. Plate Migration
Early Silurian 443 Million Years Ago (Ma BP)

While it still remained stationary, a number of micro-plates broke off from Gondwana and sped north-westwards up the western hemisphere, following in the path of Avalonia. These were Armorica, Iberia, and Alpinia, and they closed down the Rheic Ocean as they crossed it, opening up the Theic Ocean behind them.

The new super-continent of Laurussia - formed from our North America, Europe, and Asia - started to assemble itself. The gap between Avalonia and Laurentia continued to close at a northward-dipping subduction zone between the two plates.

Avalonia (present day England, Wales and Ireland) was, by this time, within 25° of the equator, experiencing a warm sub-tropical climate.

Baltica joined up with Siberia as the final stages of the Iapetus closure took place, with continuing Caledonian mountain building.

It is interesting to note that, while all this activity was going on in the present Atlantic region, on the other side of the globe, where the Pacific is now, the crust that is presently the Antarctic was sitting firmly over the equator.

Map 6. Early Devonian 418 Million Years Ago (Ma BP)

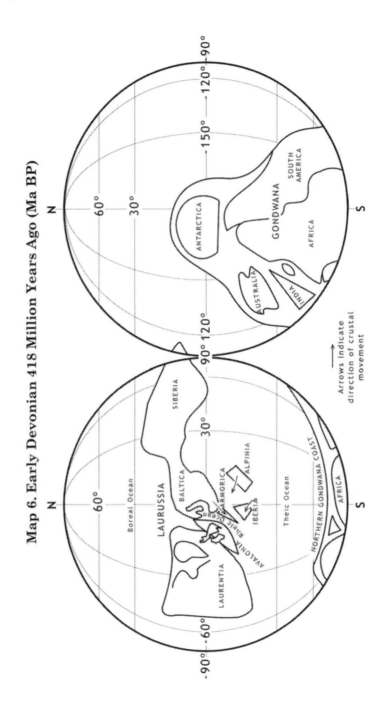

Arrows indicate direction of crustal movement

Map 6. Plate Migration
Early Devonian 418 Million Years Ago (Ma BP)

By early Devonian times, the Avalonian Plate had finally closed up hard against the Laurentian Plate, eliminating the Iapetus Ocean, and joining what was to become Scotland and northern Ireland to what was to become England and southern Ireland. The approximate shapes of the British Isles and Ireland are drawn on the Laurentia/Avalonia junction on Plate Migration Map 6. They have been drawn a little larger than to true scale, in order to make them more visible.

Much later, when, for reasons of changing mantle convection currents in the Jurassic, Laurentia started to move away from Baltica and Avalonia, the junction that had formed between them during the Devonian (called the Iapetus Suture), did not open up. Instead, the rupture took place further to the west, running through present-day Iceland, leaving the future British Isles intact and attached to Baltica.

The Caledonian mountain building ceased and was rapidly followed by the Acadian orogeny caused by the Armorican micro-plate moving in a south-westerly direction towards the southern edge of Avalonia, and narrowing the Rheic Ocean.

At long last, in late Devonian times, the changed Mantle convection currents started to move the great Gondwana super-continent, which had been stationary since late Pre-Cambrian times - a period of approximately 180 million years. Gondwana started to retrace its steps, moving south in the eastern hemisphere, crossing the south pole, and travelling northward into the western hemisphere.

Map 7. Early Carboniferous 362 Million Years Ago (Ma BP)

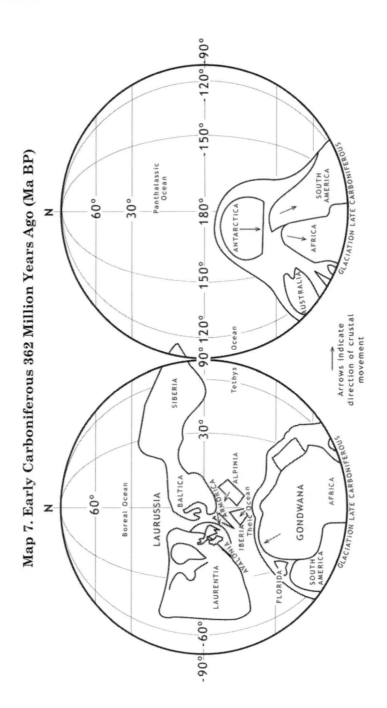

28

Map 7. Plate Migration
Early Carboniferous 362 Million Years Ago (Ma BP)

By this time, Laurentia, Avalonia, Baltica, and Siberia were spread out along the equator in the western hemisphere. Terrestrial plant life was accelerating rapidly in its evolution and quantity, so across the humid tropical zone rain forests established themselves and the world's first major coal deposits were formed.

During the Devonian, Gondwana had already moved a considerable distance towards Laurentia and Baltica, and was now rapidly narrowing the Theic Ocean between itself and the Iberia and Alpinia micro-plates.

Throughout the entire Carboniferous, as Gondwana moved further north, a 40 million years long glacial episode - the Karoo Ice Age - took place in the southern hemisphere. The centre of glacial spreading was, interestingly, offset significantly from the then south pole. Consequently, it affected what is now South America, Africa, India, and Australia. Indications of this glaciation can be observed today in both lithological and fossil evidence. The various glacial surges and retreats lowered and raised sea levels, thus creating the cyclical nature of Carboniferous sedimentation worldwide.

There has been no other ice age between then and now, which raises the possibility that our current 2.6 million years old Quaternary ice age could last for another 37 million years!

During the Carboniferous the European landmass consolidated as Iberia, and Alpinia finally closed onto Armorica, generating the Variscan mountain building orogeny, which started in Eastern Europe in the Devonian, reached Avalonia by mid-Carboniferous times, building up to its peak towards the end of the Carboniferous, but lasting into the early Permian.

Map 8. Early Permian 292 Million Years Ago (Ma BP)

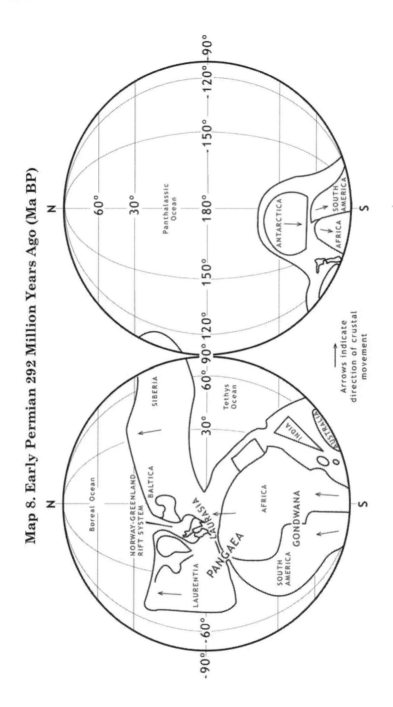

Arrows indicate direction of crustal movement

Map 8. Plate Migration
Early Permian 292 Million Years Ago (Ma BP)

Having been pretty well stationary for a considerable time, Laurentia, Baltica, and Siberia found themselves moving northwards once more. However, Gondwana, moving into the western hemisphere was travelling northwards even faster.

Eventually, therefore, the Gondwana land mass caught up with Laurasia and gently met it so that no major mountain building occurred at that time. This union created a huge single super-continent which is called Pangaea, and which existed for about 90 million years through the Permian and Triassic, with some two thirds of the globe then being covered by the Tethys, Boreal and Panthalassic Oceans.

Plate Migration Map 8 shows that the incipient breaking zone between Laurentia and Baltica manifested itself on the western side of the Norway-Greenland Rift System, running west of the British Isles and Ireland, and allowing seas to open up in Europe, but without a connection to the Tethys Ocean. This can also be seen on the main Permian and Triassic Period maps.

Looking at Plate Migration Map 8, it is possible to discern the beginnings of the shapes and positioning of the modern continents. South America and Africa are aligned and orientated, ready for the Atlantic to form, India has orientated itself in preparation for its northward journey to meet Siberia and form the Himalayas, and in the newly-forming Pacific ocean region, Antarctica starts to slide itself southwards into its present location over the south pole.

Map 9. Early Triassic 251 Million Years Ago (Ma BP)

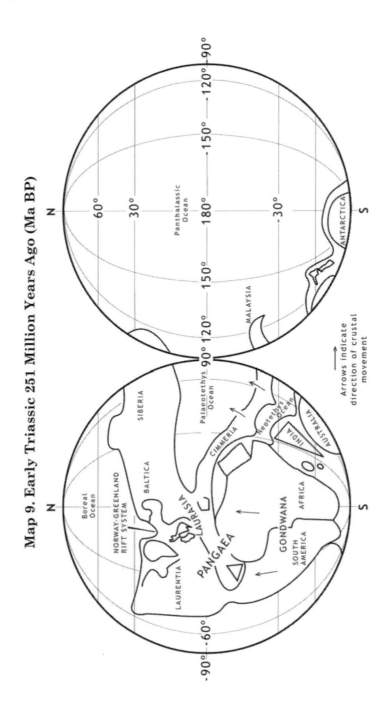

Map 9. Plate Migration
Early Triassic 251 Million Years Ago (Ma BP)

By this time, the English, French, and Spanish crustal blocks had settled in much the same relative positions as they occupy today. Similarly, the Sahara Platform was close to Spain, with a proto-Mediterranean Sea forming between the two. Europe was experiencing intense faulting and rifting as the micro-plates jostled for position, and the part of the crust that is now the British Isles rotated clockwise more towards its present north-south alignment.

The Triassic saw the beginnings of the break-up of Gondwana after 350 million years. A new set of mantle convection currents peeled off a huge strip from the east Gondwana coast, creating the immensely long peninsula of Cimmeria. This divided the Tethys Ocean into the Palaeotethys and the Neotethys, and swept its way rapidly northwards to attach itself to the southern part of Siberia to create the larger land mass of Eurasia, extending south eastwards as far as the present Malaysian peninsula.

At the end of the Triassic, marking the Triassic-Jurassic boundary, a steady 20 million year long extinction event took place with up to 80% of all the planet's species dying out.

Map 10. Early Jurassic 205 Million Years Ago (Ma BP)

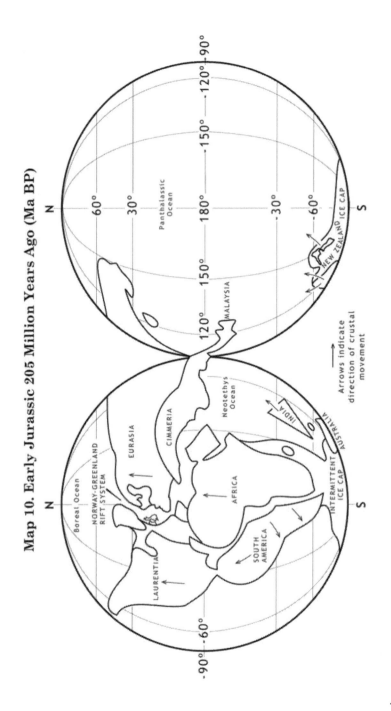

Arrows indicate
direction of crustal
movement

Map 10. Plate Migration
Early Jurassic 205 Million Years Ago (Ma BP)

As the age of the dinosaurs slowly built up to its peak, the mantle convection currents switched once again, creating an approximately east-west tension, which started the slow process of breaking up Pangaea. South America started to split away from Africa, and the split migrated northwards through the junction between Laurentia and Eurasia, and up the western side of the unstable Norway-Greenland Rift System - although the tension would not start to significantly widen this rift zone until the late Cretaceous.

Closer to home, the split ran to the west of Ireland, cutting the Avalonian Plate in half, such that the western part of that plate now formed the Atlantic provinces of north-east America and Greenland. Slowly, the UK adopted its present-day orientation.

The whole of Pangaea, although splitting east-west, was still progressing northwards, leaving Antarctica behind to settle down stationary over the south pole. India broke free as the tension built up in that region, and commenced a long northward flight across the Neotethys Ocean, heading for Cimmeria, which was now permanently lodged along the southern margin of Eurasia. Interestingly, from the point of view of bio-migrations, the European regional tensions allowed the re-linking of the Boreal Ocean to the Neotethys Ocean. Australia and New Zealand started to break free from their association with the now-fragmenting Gondwana, to later drift northwards towards their present positions in the huge Panthalassic Ocean, being 50% bigger than today's Pacific!

There is evidence of an intermittent polar ice cap over Antarctica, but not a major period of glaciation.

Map 11. Early Cretaceous 146 Million Years Ago (Ma BP)

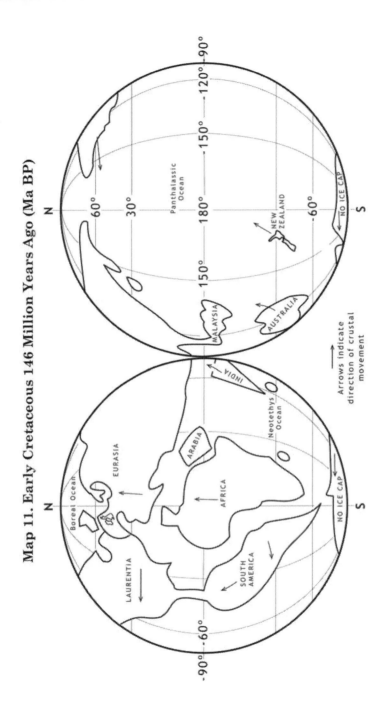

Arrows indicate direction of crustal movement

36

Map 11. Plate Migration
Early Cretaceous 146 Million Years Ago (Ma BP)

The Southern Atlantic had formed and was widening, with the split inexorably spreading northwards. The crust in the region of the British Isles and Ireland had returned to being continental up to the later Cretaceous. For most of this Period, therefore, there was a significant land bridge separating the new North Atlantic from the old Boreal Ocean.

The long westward drift of North and South America started to lead to the gentle folding of their western coastal regions and the accumulation of sediments ready for the forthcoming Alpine mountain building period, which would, in 30 million years, thrust up the Rockies and the Andes mountain ranges.

Eurasia continued drifting northwards, with Africa following on behind. South America continued to migrate northwards as well as continuing its westwards journey.

Australia had by now detached itself from Antarctica and was travelling toward the equator, whilst India approached Asia prior to its imminent hard collision to form the Himalayas.

By the end of the Cretaceous, the last of the major long-term life extinctions had built up to and passed its peak, wiping out - right at the end, and amongst others - the ammonites and dinosaurs (with the exception of birds, who are their only surviving descendants). About 76% of all existing species at the time are considered to have become extinct.

Map 12. Early Palaeogene 65 Million Years Ago (Ma BP)

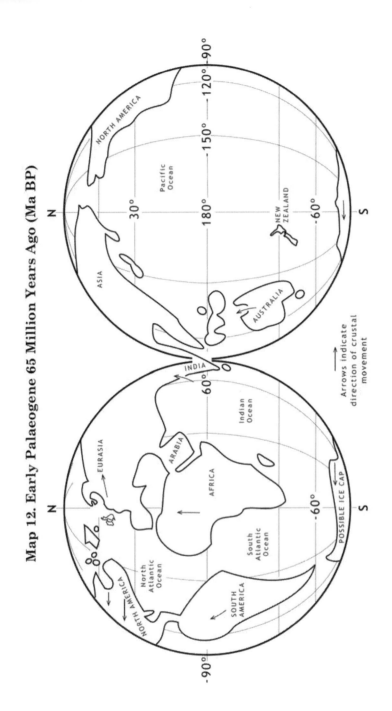

Map 12. Plate Migration
Early Palaeogene 65 Million Years Ago (Ma BP)

India finally reached Asia with a hard impact that started to drive up the Himalayan Mountains.

North and South America approached their present latitudes, still driving westwards, with gentle rippling on their western coasts, pending the onset of the main Alpine Mountain building orogeny towards the later part of the Palaeogene.

At last, the North Atlantic Ocean opened up properly and widened, splitting biotic communities and forcing them along separate courses of evolution.

The continents took on shapes much like those of the present day, with new plates forming and growing, such as the new oceanic crust on each side of the central Atlantic ridge - see Plate Migration Map 13.

It is appropriate to reflect that, although it has not been marked on the earlier maps, there must have been a Pacific Plate, possibly preceded by a huge Panthalassic Plate. These plates carried no continents on them, and so their past movements can only be geologically conjectured as being similar to those of today's Pacific Ocean, as shown on Plate Migration Map 13. Today we can make isolated and limited measurements of the movements of the oceanic floors from the development of migrating volcanic island chains created by mantle plume hot spots.

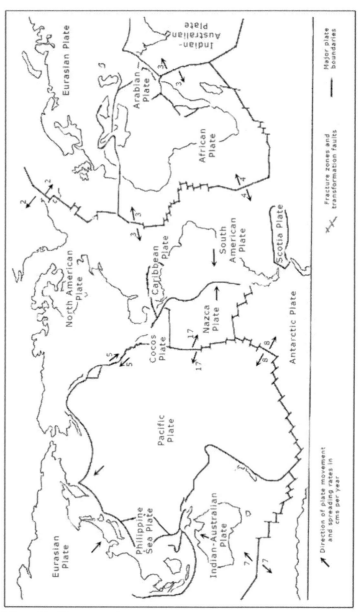

Map 13. Present Day.

Map 13. Plate Migration
Present Day

And so we arrive at the present day. What is shown here is our best current assessment of the crustal plates covering the earth today - as determined by fifty years or so of research and field experience, built up once the old idea of continental drift had evolved into the concept of plate tectonics.

This detailed map shows tectonic plates that interlock on the surface of the Earth's viscous, slowly flowing mantle.

The North and South American plates are still moving westward, but are in collision with the Pacific and Nazca plates respectively. This collision is still raising the Rocky Mountains and the Andes Mountains, although at a lesser rate than during the main Alpine orogeny. India still bears onto Asia, keeping the Himalayas still rising slowly. The Atlantic Ocean continues to widen at the rate of 3 to 4 cm per year.

As may be seen on the map, most plates are only partially covered by continental material (for example the South American and African plates have grown as the Atlantic has widened). And it may be observed that some plates (for example the Pacific and Nazca plates) exist without any major continents on them at all.

This map is also interesting because the arrows drawn on it give an indication of the direction and speed of movement or growth of different plates in centimetres per year.

Of course, as we look at the map of today's plates with their interacting boundaries, we may enjoy its simplicity but we cannot forget what we have seen in the plate tectonic maps of the distant past. We must ask ourselves, "What happened to the old plate boundaries, where plates once met, where mountain ranges once were formed, and which were eroded and buried so that we don't see them any more?"

This is a very good question, and a very important one. It is one that is at the forefront of modern tectonic research work, using some of the world's fastest super-computers to emulate the past and examine and bring to life the possibilities.

For example, we know that the ancient Avalonian/Laurentian plate junction (called the Iapetus Suture) still lies buried 12 kilometres deep beneath the Southern Upland Hills of today's Scotland. The question that should be on our minds is clear: if this ancient junction line, this ancient subduction zone scar, still exists, then what effect does it have on the current Eurasian plate of which it is part? Is it truly fossilised, or is it a line of weakness that still, after 420 million years, contributes to seismic activity and, in the event of a change in the local mantle current directions, would it perhaps provide a line of weakness to be exploited and ruptured by huge crustal forces?

After all, we know that when the mantle currents reversed, causing the creation of the Atlantic Ocean, the Iapetus Suture did not reactivate, but rather, the induced tensile stress ripped the crust apart to the west of the British Isles and Ireland, to travel through the present day Iceland region instead. We need to ask why that might have been. It is a question that cannot be ignored. And, it is a question that can be asked many times across the world in relation to ages-old crustal activity of the past. The answer creeps into our mind that perhaps, within the Laurentian plate, there was an already-existing line of weakness from an even earlier tectonic mountain building

42

event that was exploited by the tension instead of the Iapetus Suture. It is also interesting to observe in the modified world map below, that current research work indicates that there are, indeed, several ancient buried tectonic scars running down through the old Laurentian shield plate. So the idea that has crept into our mind could well be correct.

Or, alternatively, let's look at Plate Migration Map 10, still in the Jurassic, and see that over on the eastern edge of our hemisphere, Cimmeria has just made a hard impact collision with the Eurasian plate. And below that, we see that India is about to do the same. That is shown on Plate Migration Map 12, where India's hard collision with Cimmeria has already taken place. What, we have to ask, has happened to the sutures formed when those two collisions occurred? The answer is that they are still there, in the form of relic sutures or relic scars, still capable of generating seismic activity, and still potentially capable of forming a line of weakness in any forthcoming change in the Earth's mantle's convection patterns.

So, there we have three or four examples of the importance of these relic scars in the present and future behaviour of the crustal plates, and their potential effects on plate tectonics.

It is important to note that current research work in the field is suggesting very strongly that these scars are not just scars in the buckled and subducted crust of collided plates, but that they actually go deeper than that, to form relic scars within the Earth's mantle itself.

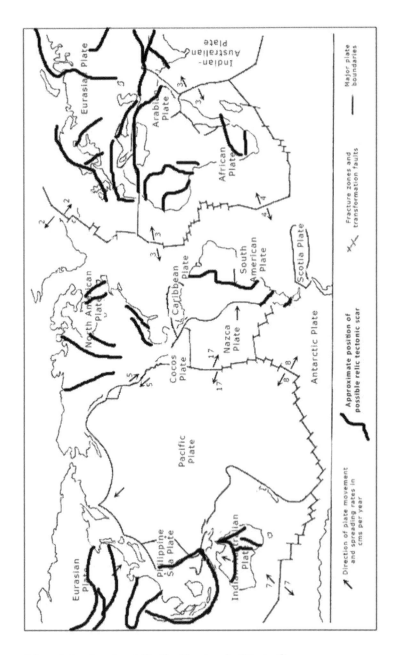

Map 14. Ancient Relic Tectonic Plate Scars.

44

But, we cannot just look at the scars we can now define from the last 540 million years. We must necessarily conjecture that there must be examples of relic scars from older, and still older tectonic plate collisions in the past, and the latest research work increasingly confirms that this is so. In this regard, the reader should note the published work by Heron and his colleagues in the reading list at the end of this book.

Thus, in Migration Map 14, let us together take a brief look at the possibilities for buried relic tectonic scars from the distant past. We can do this by examining the few that we can see from the thirteen plate migration maps submitted in this book. Then we can project that information backwards through time, in the true geological manner of 'what we see today must have happened in the past'. On the time scales we are considering, this may not always have been true, but for our purposes, it is sufficiently true to extrapolate backwards an unspecified, but very long time.

The Toronto and Aberdeen researchers cited in the reading list have combined their knowledge of basement geology, with the speed and patience of modern super-computers to look way back into the possible past, to ferret out those scenarios that carry a likelihood of having existed, and to produce the information that we can muse upon today. Professionals can use this in the furtherance of their understanding of earthquakes and vulcanism.

Map 14, above, shows the approximate position of a number of the relic tectonic scars that the computers are suggesting lie within and beneath existing tectonic plates today.

Conclusions

How much do the Plate Migration maps show the actual picture of the state of the planet's crust at those particular times?

To help us to answer this question, we must apply the principles of uniformitarianism - the belief that the processes we see about us today have always operated in the same way.

It is clear - based on the uniformitarian principles of geological observation - that the maps prepared in this book are too simple to reflect the reality of those times in that they are lacking any indication of where the plates might have interlocked beneath the world's oceans to form ocean spreading junctions where new oceanic crust was created. These are not indicated because, by-and-large, we have insufficient information on them.

We may therefore - based upon the complexity we see in Plate Migration Maps 13 and 14 - reasonably assume that all the maps 1 to 12 should contain much more complex plate structures with growth and subduction margins about which we know nothing.

Geologists have done their best to piece together the World's history from the clues in the rocks, but our knowledge of the past will never be as detailed or as reliable as our knowledge of the Earth today.

Some closing words from the author

Well, I really hope that you have enjoyed my book and your journey into the long-ago past.

We have looked across 750 million years, and have seen entire continents travel south over the face of the planet to form the great landmass of Gondwana. Then we watched as Gondwana broke up and the travelling continental plates moved back north again to coalesce into the great single continent of Pangaea. At this time there was only one continent on the planet. But, this didn't last forever, and subsequently, the great Pangaea split up as the Atlantic Ocean formed and the Americas drifted away westwards to their present positions.

We would be justified in assuming that at some far distant future time, the moving plates will re-form to create yet another great super-continent.

The timescale diagram provided in this book shows that, as the continents moved, simple cellular life forms transformed into creatures with shells and carapaces. These evolved into fish, and then amphibia and finally animals and plants that moved onto the land. Then the plants spread over the surface of our planet, filling the atmosphere with increasing quantities of oxygen, which in turn allowed reptiles, and the great dinosaurs of the Jurassic and Cretaceous to evolve.

One can be dismayed and saddened that five great mass extinctions repeatedly wiped out nearly all life on Earth, but we can rejoice together that, despite such staggering carnage, life bounced back time after time, with new species relentlessly evolving to fill the vacant niches left behind by Nature's devastation.

We have watched the great crustal plates move inexorably across the Earth's surface, to collide with one another, creating four major periods of mountain building over the last five hundred million years.

Finally, the great northern ice sheets of the Quaternary period have carved the landscapes of the northern continents ready for the evolution of the human race; landscapes that we know and love today.

Our study of plate migrations did not even touch on the evolution of humans and their effects on the planet. That was all too brief for our geological time scales - all of humankind's ten thousand years of civilisation a mere blink of a geological eye.

Perhaps, having shared this great adventure together, we can wonder how long or how brief our own evolutionary story might be. Some types of animal, including dinosaurs, spiders, and fish have populated the planet for hundreds of millions of years without change, and most have died out. We can only wonder with awe at the scale of life, and ask, "how will we evolve? What will we be like in another fifty million years? Or will we simply have become extinct also?"

Are we just one intelligent species among tens of thousands of others spread across our galaxy, or are we alone?

I have enjoyed travelling with you, and I hope that you, too, have enjoyed our journey together through an almost unimaginably long stretch of time.

Peter Roberts.

P.S. if you have enjoyed your journey with me, please tell me by emailing me at peter.roberts@russetpublishing.com

READING LIST

"The Geology of England and Wales" 2nd Edition (2006)
Edited: P. J. Brenchley and P. F. Rawson
Published: The Geological Society of London
ISBN: 978-1-86239-200-7

"The Geology of England and Wales." (1992)
Edited: P. McL. D. Duff and A. J. Smith
Published: The Geological Society of London
ISBN: 978-0-903317-70-2

"The Geology of Scotland" 4th Edition (2003)
Author: N. H. Trewin
Published: The Geological Society of London
ISBN: 1-86239-126-2

"Atlas of Palaeogeography and Lithofacies" (1999)
Edited: J. C. W. Cope, J. K. Ingham, and P. F. Rawson
Published: The Geological Society of London
ISBN: 978-1-862390-55-3

"Intraplate orogenesis within accreted and scarred lithosphere:
Example of the Eurekan Orogeny, Ellesmere Island",
Heron, P., Pysklywec R. N., and Stephenson R.,
Tectonophysics, 664, 202-213, 2015.
Joint research projects on tectonic scars, by:
Universities of Toronto, Canada, and Aberdeen, Scotland.

Keywords: *geology, palaeogeography, historical geology, evolution, climate change, climatology, global warming, plate tectonics, continental drift, maps, atlas, oceanography, meteorology, fossils, mass extinctions, mountain building, orogeny.*

Printed in Great Britain
by Amazon